How To Find Your Soulmate

The Best Dating Advice For Women Strategies For Attracting Men And Discovering Your Soul mate

(Finding Your Life Mate And Soul Mate)

Leopoldo Scott

TABLE OF CONTENT

Make Yourself Available to Date?.. 1

Trying to picture your ideal soul partner 8

The Solution Is Here 13

How to Tell If You've Found Your Soulmate.............48

The ideal partners may be brought together through matchmakers..52

Exactly what guys want in a partner 57

Where to Look Online for Your Soulmate..................79

The Best Ways to Make an Online Profile..................82

The Relationships and the Law of Attraction...........99

You As well Enjoy Musical Theater? 109

To find self-love, be clear..129

Avoid common relationship blunders......................140

Player Tendencies 162

MAKE YOURSELF AVAILABLE TO DATE?

How often do we hear people claim that they can never meet someone suitable for dating? Despite their best efforts, which include regularly checking online dating websites, accepting invites from friends, and joining several groups, they never manage to meet someone with whom they really click. Is anything else going on or are they really ready, willing to date, and unflappable in their search?

If so, what must occur for you to make yourself available for a date?

Work might put a lot of demands and restrictions on our availability to date. We may not have much free time or energy to enthusiastically make the effort to look attractive and be receptive to someone else's attractions if we are exhausted, preoccupied, or overcommitted. When we're engrossed in work demands, deadlines, and family obligations, there isn't usually much time, money, or effort left over to prepare for a new encounter.

In the next weeks and months, we may not even know how free we will be to fully pursue a new relationship. Working long hours or spending a lot of time away from home might hinder our desire to date. Even contemplating the early stages of a new relationship might seem like too much work since we are already so busy. However, creating a company or career is often done with an eye toward our future expectations, anticipating settling down with a partner, starting a family, and co-constructing a home.

Carefully seeking a better balance in life often involves a mental shift in which we include all aspects of life and make ourselves available for dating.

Friends who know us well may say that they truly want to see us settled and loved-up in a wonderful new relationship, but is that actually the case? Are you certain that they understand the dynamics of your relationship changing, where your time and devotion may start to be influenced by the need to consider someone else?

As they begin to depend on you more, or as they start to be critical of any potential new suitor, you can notice a change in their behavior. Pay attention to what is happening and attempt to communicate how you are both feeling. Give assurance that they will always be important and decide to maintain regular communication, even if it must sometimes be conducted over the phone or online.

Family may be an engaging topic, especially if you have deep ties to your parents or siblings. Siblings may be excited about the idea of their brother or sister dating, particularly if they've shared a lot, helped one another through difficult times, survived a breakup, and spent a lot of time together sharing confidances and advice while regularly checking in.

Mother and daughters. Girls often claim that their mother is their best friend; they talk to each other every day and discuss everything. But there is a proverb that reads, Give your children roots to grow and wings to soar. Some moms find it difficult to let go and rely excessively on their daughters for companionship. They can be fearful of losing their intense bond with a new third party.

If a mother won't let her child go, she may sabotage the possibility of her daughter establishing a new relationship. She may often be in a position of influence where she is always presenting herself with money, treats, and inside information. She could make frequent phone calls and is always willing to help and provide support at a moment's notice. How can a possible new relationship compete with such a strong, deep connection?

Sons and fathers are often wonderful companions, sharing interests and hobbies, maybe spending hours together over a shared love of sports, cars, and other things. Some people may mesh well and become excellent partners. A new lady friend might significantly interfere with how much time they typically choose to spend together. As with mothers and daughters, it might be difficult to walk away if the father is determined to win back your affection and plays the "why marry him or her" card hard.

Accept that the change must come from you if you've begun to realize how much you're struggling to make yourself available to date. You must determine if something is right or wrong. Any new relationship requires work, compromise, and may sometimes seem like hard work.

Some things may need to alter if you ultimately want to settle down, maybe locate a long-term company, or even create a family. You may well need to take the step of becoming firmer and more forceful in some of your current relationships. You must be willing to put up the effort necessary to mentally, physically, and emotionally prepare yourself to meet someone who will satisfy your relationship needs. Then, you'll be able to go on dates!

TRYING TO PICTURE YOUR IDEAL SOUL PARTNER

Undoubtedly one of our most underutilized natural talents is creativity. Despite the fact that it is essential to how we shape the situations in life. When it comes to imagination, we often imagine an artist. A painting or sculpture will first be imagined by the artist in their mind's eye before being physically created.

With everything in life, whether on purpose or accidentally, we behave in the same way. Purposeful creation is the difference between success and failure. Your chances of finding the soulmate or connection you want increase with more clearly you see your ideal partner. How long have you been daydreaming about meeting your soul mate? Not at all, if you are like most people! We believe that our ideas are meaningless and that they have no bearing on how our lives develop, especially when it comes to meeting our soul match.

Imagine the kind of person you want to be with, and the universe will have a template to fill in the specifics of what you want. It's a good idea to start by taking 10 peaceful minutes when you may concentrate on the person of your dreams. And it helps to enjoy the process while trying to picture your soul partner. Enjoy yourself while you visualize the person of your dreams.

It's crucial to feel positive when you're visualizing. You will be more in harmony with your ambition and with life if you, for instance, invest more love into your appearance. Let that picture go after that. The imaginative component also requires not trying. Over-efforting might stifle creative thought. Gain the ability to visualize with ease and lightness. Making a lot of effort to make anything happen slows down the whole process. Give it a "try." You could find that not trying goes against your upbringing.

The mirror of life is for you. Examining your connections with the people in your life is one of the simplest methods to determine whether you are in tune with the creative process of finding a soulmate. Do you generally like interacting with people? Although you won't get along with everyone in your life, you could discover that you do with the majority of people.

Through the Law of Attraction, everyone we come into contact with, whether it be at work, a sporting event, or just while driving down the street, reflects the energy that we are being. Everybody is a reflection of you. The reflection might be lovely or ugly depending on the situation.

The key is in your ability to influence how life reflects back to you. Would you prefer to hang out with someone like you? Even though we might be our own worst critics at times, you definitely have a lot of amazing inner qualities that others find appealing.

A crucial first step is to evaluate your contribution to a partnership. I am aware that I did it. And it plays a significant role in luring a soul mate. You don't even need to have a large list of the good qualities you exhibit. It may just consist of two or three elements. The Law of Attraction is the key, as always. You'll draw more of what you concentrate on. You will start to draw in others who have higher vibrations as you "vibrate" to these aspects of yourself. Since everything is energy, it is crucial to approach relationships from an energetic perspective.

If you have a positive outlook on life, you will attract positive individuals. You will draw other angry individuals to you if you are angry yourself. Life is all about making decisions. If you make the decision to be happy no matter what, life will only provide you with positive people and situations.

You may set the scene for positive things to happen to you, including encounters with positive individuals, if you build a momentum of positive thinking. You only need to choose what you will be and be that; you don't need to strive to achieve anything. The rest is taken care of by life. But all you have to do is react to the situations that arise. So, the FedEx guy or woman won't necessarily knock on your door if you desire a fantastic relationship.

THE SOLUTION IS HERE

Without severing her gaze from her partner for even a second, Monica flicked her hair over her shoulder. She put on her sexiest grin and gently moved her hips as the book had instructed her. might you be open to a suggestion that might make Spring Break the finest ever, Gary?

He had previously informed her that he had no desire to spend Spring Break at the beach. But it was her fault for approaching it incorrectly. She now realized that all she needed to do was ask him the proper question.

He grinned. You may ask me anything when I'm wearing that outfit.

Monica gave herself a mental high five. What a wonderful idea to purchase and wear a trendy new outfit! Why hadn't she come up with the idea herself?

Gary moved closer and placed his arms over her shoulders.

I live next to a neighbor who owns a timeshare.

Gary lowered his hands and scowled. "Monica. I'm not interested in visiting the beach. It had a serious tone.

Monica inhaled deeply. She had no intention of giving up. She continued to smile as she licked her lips and sagged her hip to one side. You have no idea to what you are saying "no." Straight from the direct sales company's training DVD, which she had just joined.

Gary began to smile. What exactly am I refusing to now?

Monica moved to close the little space between them. "He's going to give us free lodging." Yet another marketing plan. Assume that the consumer has already made the decision to purchase the product. "Consider it." She spoke more softly while fluttering her eyelids. "I and you. 6 days. we're all by ourselves in a timeshare.

Gary bent down, placed his hands back on her shoulders, and gave her a kiss. Hard. He backed away and remarked, "Sounds great." His arms were then crossed. "He's coughing up the airline tickets, too?"

"Gary!" In her whining, she tried to seem as innocent as possible.

Gary shook his head and scowled once again. Monny, "No dice. You know I need the cash for my next semester's tuition, right?

Monica was now enraged. "Fine. This Spring Break, I will be the sole female who has nothing planned. I believed you to adore me. She shoved him in the chest as she spoke this last phrase.

Gary grabbed her arm and forcefully squeezed it. "I believed you to love me." He let go of her arm, and she caressed it while wiping tears from her eyes. You just love yourself, however. He whirled around. Find another victim to exploit. I've left the area.

******

The issue with the majority of relationship books is that they teach you how to manipulate others to obtain what you want, as I alluded to in the start. That fits right in with how our society is now since manipulation is a common technique.

Parents use coercion to encourage their kids to act a specific way; they refer to this as "discipline". The public is tricked by advertisers into purchasing their goods (they refer to this as "marketing"). Teachers use deception to attempt to motivate their pupils to work harder (they refer to this as "motivation"). Employers use threats to coerce workers into working longer hours and for less compensation (I'm not sure what employers refer to as "threatening" behavior).

Not only is manipulation a common behavior, but for many individuals it has also developed into a harmful habit. It certainly is awful. Do you want somebody to bribe, threaten, lie to, and lie to you to force you to do something you wouldn't normally do? Do you agree with that?

But everyone who lives in the current world experiences it on a daily basis, and you are just as guilty of manipulation as anybody else. So am I. It takes a lifetime to attempt to rid our bodies of choleric folks, who are the worst. The best we can aspire for is a significant improvement before we pass away.

However, something isn't always appropriate simply because you have a specific mentality or because everyone else does it. For a moment, I'm going to assume that I'm your mother and ask, "Would you jump off a bridge if everyone else did?" particularly if the bridge simply resulted in additional heartbreak?

I didn't believe that. Instead of learning about obscure methods that will ultimately just make your life worse, you're here to learn about what really works in finding your soul partner.

Religious works are not exempt.

I should make this clear to my readers who profess some belief in a personal God: some Christian writers engage in deceit as well. Return to the scenario where Monica asks Gary whether he would be interested in hearing a certain concept. I discovered it from a Christian author; it's a unique method for influencing someone's viewpoint.

Following that, there are the "Five Love Languages." It's important to recognize the many ways that individuals express their love, including via acts of kindness, presents, and other acts of service, but there is a narrow line between using these actions to express love and using them to manipulate others. To encourage your spouse to agree to what you want, for instance, you could find that he responds to love the most when he receives presents.

Being the straightforward choleric that I am, I immediately insisted that Jerry assist me in the kitchen more after finishing that book since that is how I primarily experience love. Keep in mind the phrase "demanded." Demanding something is an obvious, overt, and direct kind of manipulation. Plain and simple, a demand is a disguised threat.

So after doing the dishes a few times, he became very angry. On the other hand, I made the decision that I needed to start purchasing Jerry little presents if I wanted to have the greatest marriage possible (the book claims that loving people by speaking their "language" can improve marriages). Being a natural cheapskate who despises seeing money spent on items I don't really need, I quickly started to dislike that. And I detest coming up with present ideas for folks. I lack the ability to go into a shop and instantly know that an item is the perfect fit for a certain customer.

In essence, I was attempting to influence the course of our relationship for the better. Did it succeed? We are happy than ever since I stopped asking Jerry to assist me with cleaning a few weeks later. I also stopped giving him pointless presents and cards years ago.

I'm not claiming that the book's author intended for people to exploit his material to influence them. Just pointing out how simple it is to do so. Particularly for those who are sticklers for detail and demand perfection.

Communication, not manipulation, is the key.

The farthest an action may be from love is manipulation. And if you say or do things you wouldn't normally say or do only to attempt to "make" a guy change, you will ultimately lose your heart, one way or another.

Learn to communicate instead of manipulate if you're serious about meeting your true match. Any enduring, fulfilling relationship is built on communication. I don't mean "communication" in the manner that ladies blab on and on about every aspect of their day when I say that. You can speak nonstop and never get anything through. Two-way communication is essential. It requires at least two parties, with the recipient comprehending the essence of the message the sender is attempting to convey.

Communication in a love relationship is mostly about initially connecting and then strengthening the relationships between the two people. Even if doing so may spark natural dialogue, this cannot be accomplished by sitting down together and answering a series of questions from a relationship manual. Instead, connecting and bonding take place when you have genuine dialogue. You must master a number of communication skills in order to do so in a manner that will improve your connection. They apply to your friendships as well as to love relationships. Learning the following abilities will greatly enhance and enrich your life overall, not only in the field of romance, if you have trouble establishing and retaining friends generally.

1. Be truthful about your views.

This does not mean that you should share all 10,000 of your thoughts and opinions with a possible partner on the first date. This would be the explanation if you have a habit of doing it and never get a second date. Information overload is disliked by everyone, particularly males. Additionally, you run the risk of frightening the person you want to fall in love with.

We are all going through a growing process. You could change your mind about what you believe tomorrow. What's more important to our topic here is that your partner's beliefs will evolve with time. They may not now share a belief that is really important to you, but after spending time with you and communicating honestly, they might start to do so.

Let me relate one of my own experiences. I was certain that Creation occurred precisely as the Bible claims it did when I first met Jerry. I wasn't raised a literalist, but by the time I was in my mid-twenties, I was. But Jerry thought the early writings of the Bible had far more symbolic truth than factual reality. We started talking about it later in our marriage, and I started to see his perspective. I am not persuaded that it is possible to establish that God created the world in seven days, but I am also not convinced that it is possible to claim with certainty that God could not have done so.

What if, on our first date, I had brought up the matter and insisted that Jerry share my viewpoint or we would have to part ways? What would have happened? I would still be unmarried and would not have wed my true love!

This first skill is not about overwhelming someone with your opinions on every topic you've ever considered, nor is it about forcing him to choose between you and his own personal convictions. (This latter scenario, by the way, would constitute manipulation.) The ability is more about being truthful in your responses and knowing when to stop.

Tell the truth when he asks what you think about horses if you are scared of them and you are aware that the guy you are interested in loves horses. You two may be able to coexist in great happiness even if neither of you ever changes your stance on that matter.

Keep in mind that being honest does not equate to being ruthless in the same spirit. Answer the question politely and concisely. Avoid arguing, have an open mind, and refrain from attempting to convince him to see things your way. Without a doubt, you will fail. Keep in mind that everyone, including yourself, is traveling on their own trip and that it is impossible to meet someone who shares your precise beliefs on all matters.

On the other side, you need to be aware of when your ideas may conflict to the point that they are likely to lead to issues in the future. No disrespect to sports addicts, but the only televised sporting event that was ever viewed in my household was the World Series. Even though my parents enjoyed baseball rather well, they never watched the regular season games since my dad detested American football.

So as I became older, I made the decision that I would never date a guy who insisted on watching every single game of every single sport that was on television. I didn't want a guy who was interested in sports since I had other interests and didn't want him to live for the next game.

I discovered one, and I am certain that our marriage is far happier now than it would have been if I had made a concession.

For many others, religion is also a deal-breaker. You should carefully evaluate the potential effects of a relationship with someone who has different spiritual views from you on your personal development, other relationships, and child-rearing choices, should you decide to have kids.

Therefore, when a possible True Love inquires about your views, be forthright but non-aggressive, and be prepared to end a relationship if the man has values that conflict with yours — regardless of how nice his butt may be.

What about former romantic consorts? How forthcoming should you be? whether the man asks whether you're a virgin, tell him the truth, but don't go into detail if you're not. Similar rules apply if you've ever had a different partner, been engaged, or been married. If he doesn't inquire about your prior love relationships, withhold any information.

You shouldn't inquire about his background either. The rationale for this is because such knowledge may cause unwarranted resentment or serve as fuel for future confrontations. Of course, the other has a right to know whether one of you has engaged in promiscuity, as well as a right to know if he or she has developed any diseases as a result of the lifestyle.

Since I've brought it up, if your boyfriend has a history of promiscuity, you need to be confident he's changed and will be devoted to you. You do realize that this book is about preventing heartbreak?

2. Disagree politely

This talent was briefly mentioned in the previous one, but it is essential for all types of communication, not simply those involving personal ideas. You will wait forever if you are looking for someone who always thinks the same as you do. Of course, the typical process of building a love connection begins with a couple identifying and praising their shared interests. In fact, a couple may even reach the stage of becoming engaged to be married or agreeing to live together before they start realizing that they really have quite different views and attitudes in various areas of life.

When this realization is initially realized, a lot of people—especially women—leave the relationship or feel inclined to do so. Like getting a smack in the face. Why do you think I detest Thai food? You like Chinese food, so I assumed you'd enjoy Thai cuisine as much as I do. Oh my God, how am I supposed to live with a Thai food hater?

Although it may sound absurd, many relationships end due of such little disagreements. Some individuals could even fail to find their soul mate as a result of their high expectations.

Asking yourself some fundamental questions is necessary when you come to the realization that Mr. Perfect isn't quite as perfect as you thought he was. How does he treat you? Do you and your partner agree on the things that are most important to you, such as your faith, kids, money, or way of life? Do you really believe that he is "the one" notwithstanding your regret because he doesn't share your opinions on food preferences (or whatever the relevant topic may be)?

then accept that you are wrong. Instead of going through a white board explanation with flow charts and diagrams to attempt to persuade him to alter his perspective on the matter, this is the most polite method to disagree with someone. Even if it works, which it typically doesn't, you run the danger of crossing the line from persuasion to manipulation. Even if he could go toward agreeing if his closest friend offered the same facts, your spouse will see you as pestering if you are married and will thus oppose your arguments. Embarrassing yet true.

3. Be open to learning new things.

Contrarily, when conflicts appear to take you in separate directions, it might result in conflict. A frequent disagreement is whether to have children and, if so, how many. Another consideration is the kind of home to buy. Then what? If your spouse is open to it, talk to them openly and logically. You may want to postpone the conversation for a day or two if you're currently having PMS. We both understand how unlikely it is for you to maintain your composure at "that time of the month"— a snowstorm in Miami in July.

When you're prepared, take turns outlining your thoughts and convictions on the matter. Pay attention to your spouse. He could have a viewpoint that you have never thought about and it just might sway you to his point of view! Remember that you both are in the midst of a lifelong growing journey and that you are not infallible. Be open to expanding your perspective and learning from the person you love. He is sometimes in the right.

What if you don't resolve your differences by the time the conversation is over? Normally, you can ignore the problem for a time. In our marriage, Jerry and I often return to a topic after thinking about it for a few days or weeks to discover that by then, we are both fervently open to making a compromise that ultimately proves to be a win-win solution.

On the other side, someone's views could be motivated by past emotional trauma. Your man's reluctance to have children, for instance, can be due to really traumatic events involving his siblings. He may need to speak to a psychologist or family therapist with you by his side in order to be able to get rid of the worry that his own children may develop into holy terrors.

Be adaptable and teachable as you and your soul mate work through any form of disagreement you may have.

connected to...

4. Remain composed.

Keep your composure when disputes arise from differences. Getting furious won't solve anything.

Time for a sincere admission: I'm a hypocrite. When Jerry and I argue, I am the worst at letting the Drama Queen within run wild. Which, since all that does is force him into his man cave, is extremely stupid. The longer we've been married, the better I've become, but I still need to improve. We were married in our mid-thirties, which hasn't helped since five years into our marriage, perimenopause came at me like a huge claw. "Increased emotional drama due to intensified hormonal changes," are you able to say?

The good news is that you can get through difficult periods when disagreement appears unending and insurmountable when you are determined to be together for better or worse. The good news is that if you can step away from the conflict for a while—saying things like, "Honey, I love you, but I can't talk about this without getting upset right now"—chances are that a day or two later, the conflict will feel much less dangerous to your sense of wellbeing and you will be able to talk it out with your partner calmly and without fuss.

4. Be succinct and to the point.

Although Matthew Cuthbert "found it rather difficult for his slower intelligence to keep up with [Anne's] brisk mental processes," as is said in the classic novel Anne of Green Gables. It's not only Matthew Cuthbert, and a man's intelligence has nothing to do with it. Male human brains exhibit simpler behavior than female brains. They concentrate on one thing at a time.

Have you ever noticed how, ten minutes after a guy asks you how your day was, you haven't even reached the middle of your colorful, thorough account, his eyes begin to glaze over? He was seeking something along the lines of, "Great! "The students were awful today," or "The boss enjoyed my presentation. All day, I questioned why I had ever believed I would like teaching. He wants a one- to three-sentence synopsis, not even the Cliff Notes version of the book you are inclined to provide.

There are times when it's OK for you to speak out your ideas. And sometimes, it's simply impossible to imagine an event without some specifics. But in order to speak to a guy successfully, you must keep your statements succinct and to the point. When he asks you about anything, he simply wants to hear about that thing and nothing else, unless it's really important for him to comprehend. Leave out any references to ABC or LMN. Keep the heated debates between God and your women.

5. Pose free-form inquiries.

This is an excellent ability to have, especially when you are first meeting someone. Don't undervalue its significance in a long-term relationship, however. No matter the relationship, whether it is between a woman and husband, a mother and kid, or two platonic friends, there is always opportunity for improvement.

A inquiry that needs more than a single word, notably "yes" or "no," is said to be open-ended. It stimulates reflection, experience sharing, and more self-disclosure in the individual being questioned.

Also, replies to open-ended inquiries are not constrained. more than "Did you like Forrest Gump?" is "Which movie do you like better, On Golden Pond or Forrest Gump?," but if Rocky is the person's all-time favorite film, you won't get that information by giving them an option. Young children or when attempting to decide which of the two types of meat in the freezer you should cook for supper should use this method. Open-ended inquiries, however, are the most effective when you want true dialogue to occur, particularly when attempting to determine if the attractive man sitting in front of you is "the one."

Since conventional education has taught most of us to hear and ask questions with a single correct response, which often consists of two to three words, they are not always simple to come up with on the spot. Who was the first President? When did the Revolutionary War occur? What is the capital of Ohio? encourage us to continue asking similar questions as adults.

When asked, "Where were you born?" What do you like reading? "When did you begin working here?" Such inquiries don't reveal anything about the real character of the person you are addressing and are one step beyond yes-or-no inquiries. Yes, asking and receiving responses to such queries is communication, although the most fundamental kind. Questions should provide a broad range of possible replies and call for more than a two-word response if you want to learn more about someone.

I want to warn you about a sad reality that I just heard about on a talk program that I happened to see while getting a root canal before I share with you some example questions you may ask a possible Life Partner. The presenter, a male, was outlining five cunning things that men do to control the discussion, if not the lady herself, on a first date.

I squirmed in the dental chair as I heard him acknowledge these things because, first of all, I didn't think Jerry would have pulled off any of those pranks on our first date or any date after that, and, second, since Jerry never did any of those things on any date after that! The talking head's assumption that all men were as sleazy as he had been in his dating days (he is now married with three teenage sons at home) didn't seem fair to me, but then again, I haven't really explored the conventional dating scene.

So it's conceivable that the man you have identified as "Mr. Right" may mature and come to see the fallacy of his deceitful behavior, but for the time being, he'll likely use at least one of those underhanded strategies. Men prefer to focus the conversation on women on first dates, according to the one thing on the list that I can still remember and that is relevant to our issue. They specifically probe the ladies to learn all about their interests before acting as if they share their interests.

Therefore, even if they themselves dislike such trips, they will arrange a trip to the symphony and a miniature golf course for later days. Of course, the goal is to win her over and make her feel more a part of his life.

Stop allowing this to happen to you! On the first date, it's okay to let the guy ask as many questions as he likes, but you should also start asking your own open-ended inquiries to keep the discussion from being exclusively about you. You may have misjudged the man and should consider this your first and last date with him if he seems uncomfortable or attempts to avoid responding.

The list of open-ended questions that may be used to get to know anybody, but especially the guy you think might be your soul mate, is provided below:

What did you like most about the community where you grew up?

"Why did you switch from being a Democrat to being a Libertarian?" (If you are able to talk about politics in a calm way)

How did viewing Forrest Gump alter your viewpoint on those with intellectual disabilities? (Yes, I enjoyed that film!)

"What five dreams would you most like to realize if you didn't have to worry about money?"

"Describe your favorite childhood vacation for me."

Tell me more about...

"Please elaborate on..."

Examples of open-ended inquiries for someone with whom you have bonded are provided below:

How may we achieve our goal of an early retirement, in your opinion?

What are the two most important things I could do to increase your sense of respect, and why?

Why did you have a change of heart towards X? (asked in a tone that is both courteous and informal!)

How can I best assist you in attaining your business, financial, health, or other goal?

What do you interpret this [book excerpt] to mean?

Tell me more about...

"Please elaborate on..."

If you grin at him when you ask him these kinds of inquiries, he'll probably provide more information than he otherwise would have.

Speaking of smiling, I want to end this chapter with the one crucial communication technique that, regardless of how successfully you use the other five techniques, may make or ruin a relationship.

6. Pay attention to your body language.

Jeff folded his arms while grinning. You are stunning in that outfit.

Candy opened her lips and lifted her brows as she stretched her arms. You are stunning in that outfit.

Jeff or Candy, who was making the sincere compliment? Which character was speaking with a voice that was undoubtedly dripping with sarcasm? Researchers have discovered that non-verbal signals play a significantly larger role in communication than words do. More than anything else, a person's body language, facial expressions, and tone of voice reveal what they are really thinking.

A guy who often folds his arms is expressing that he is on the defensive. Someone who is unable to directly address you while speaking is either very bashful, has something to conceal, or is lying. People who are anxious often shift their weight from one foot to the other, make a repetitive motion with their hands, or do both.

However, for other individuals, crossing their arms over their chest is just a comfortable position. A person who has difficulty seeing you in the eye while speaking may be preoccupied with other thoughts or impatiently anticipating another person. In order to guarantee that the recipient properly understands the information you are giving, it is important to use the right voice tone and facial expressions while speaking to someone.

Of course, in a perfect world, you learn to communicate using body language that is suitable for the situation. However, adopt the appropriate tone and facial expression if you've formed particular habits of posture and movement while speaking to others and don't want them to be misconstrued.

I was having a tough day a couple of weeks before I started writing this chapter of the book. We were remodeling a shed into our new house while living in a tiny travel trailer, and I had to get used to new habits like doing the washing by hand. Due to the fact that we were from the South and lacked sufficient clothing for the very cold, snowy, and sleety weather that arrived only a few days after we moved into our remote property, the three of us were also locked together in the trailer for almost a week.

When Jerry entered after doing some task outside, I was eager to leave the cramped "tin can" and was on the verge of tiredness.

Even though I didn't feel like being polite, I wanted to thank him for watching our kid so that I could get some work done. "Thank you for reading to Benjamin so much this morning." My tone was terse, and my face was sallow. I didn't stop what I was doing or turn to look at him.

a break. "Do you mean that, or are you being sarcastic?" was then asked.

I then realized that when I had talked, I hadn't seemed or sounded the slightest bit thankful. I said, "Oh, no, I really meant it," attempting to convey my sincerity.

Jerry seemed content. Sadly, Jerry. It's difficult for me to communicate anything other than my intensity while I'm feeling it. You may sometimes get away with that type of communication error after being married for a while. But generally speaking, if your body language, tone of voice, and facial expressions are in line with what you are saying — or attempting to convey — you will connect with your One And Only far more successfully.

***

Keep in mind that communication is essential if you want to have a long-lasting, fulfilling connection with your soul mate. More heartache will only result from manipulation.

So now you are aware of the key. You have a basic understanding of the many temperaments, how the stereotypes about men may damage relationships, and how you need to start changing in order to become more appealing.

You're prepared to go out and meet the guy you will love for the rest of your life, right?

only if you want to go through yet another heartbreak. The consequences of rushing the search for your soul mate are generally discussed in the next chapter.

HOW TO TELL IF YOU'VE FOUND YOUR SOULMATE

If you're a movie buff, you may have noticed that once the hero and heroine first meet, they somehow instantly realize that they are a couple created for each other. How we wish it were possible to recognize our genuine love or soulmate the instant we lay eyes on them in our everyday life.

We do aspire to meet our ideal partner when we begin to navigate the valleys of life. Even if we keep running across prospective soul mates, life may be harsh at times, and they all seem to shatter our hearts. The hunt is still ongoing.

Teenagers repeatedly fall in love, but as we get older we recognize that we need to get beyond such puppy love or infatuation. Sometimes we are fortunate enough to discover our genuine life mate, even while we are young and naive. He or she is the one on whose shoulder you may lay all of your cares, anxieties, joys, and pleasure. We run to them for consolation, assurance, and even just to meet and converse with them.

Here are some encouraging indications of real love: You don't have to fake or adopt an artificial demeanor in their presence since they accept you for who you are. You may weep your heart out or keep laughing because they don't mind. In fact, they could even join your mood swing. o They don't mind being corrected or reprimanded by you; they won't run away from you after a significant argument. o The sun and moon may shift places, but they will never betray their word in any way, you may be sure.

You should consider yourself very fortunate and wonderfully blessed by God that you have such a fantastic life partner by your side if your soul mate has even half of the attributes listed above.

Find your true self, which is concealed under layers of ego and false conduct, before embarking on a quest. Who are you really? What values and principles do you uphold? How loving and affectionate are you? Are you strong enough to handle genuine love? Do you have the maturity to comprehend a soul mate?

Other indications that you've found your soul partner include the following:

having a strong physical attraction to one another and sharing similar interests and activities having regard and understanding for one another making one another feel lovely and unique being pleased to keep each other company, sometimes losing sight of the outer world

You must have patience if you want to find your life spouse. Waiting for a decent person is preferable than traveling with someone unworthy of your time. Whether two souls are actually compatible and meant for each other can only be determined through time.

Take each day as it comes until that time, and let nature run its course. And if you think you've found your soul mate, silently thank God and pray that your union will continue to grow.

THE IDEAL PARTNERS MAY BE BROUGHT TOGETHER THROUGH MATCHMAKERS.

Don't hesitate to pursue a job as a matchmaker if you are thinking about it! Today, the business of matching people has grown significantly. The concept of matchmaking may be described as a method of primarily pairing up individuals for the primary goal of dating or even marriage.

Today's matchmakers operate in a very professional manner. Simply put, matchmakers are indispensable consultants that assist us in finding the ideal spouse or romantic companion. The biggest benefit of using a matchmaker is their extensive network of connections, which may help you find the ideal partner you've been looking for. Additionally, matchmakers have some decent social ties. If you're looking for a partner, this is quite helpful.

A matchmaker's primary responsibility is to unite the ideal couples. The matchmaker's role was to evaluate the suitability and compatibility of the two families. In a traditional community, when the family unit is highly valued and a breakup is often seen with disdain, matchmaking typically takes place. The link between the two groups is now even more important than the compatibility of the couple since the matchmaker is responsible for creating a calm and long-lasting relationship between the two families.

Additionally, the genuineness of the families, their history, and many other factors are heavily reliant on the matchmakers. But in some mysterious manner, the conventional idea of matching is opening the door for more advanced approaches to finding a match. When looking for their children's ideal companion, many do contact these matchmakers. Matchmakers don't even need their own offices anymore. They may establish contacts while working remotely. Start looking through a big database for your ideal mate. All things considered, we can all agree that matchmakers are skilled at uniting ideal matches.

Is the ideal mate in your future?

Are love matches predetermined in heaven, and our job as humans is to find them here on earth? Is finding the right mate a question of fate? Do stars predict your future?

life companion? These are some of the perplexing issues that prompt us to delve more into the enigmatic realm of astrology and fortune telling.

Even those who disbelieve in such hocus-pocus are interested in learning if astrological predictions are accurate. However, a lot of these assertions are supported by mathematical and scientific calculations based on your Zodiac sign and its stars. For instance, according to astrological readings, Librans are a severe no-no for Aries individuals, whereas Sagittarius and Leo are often considered ideal partners for Aries.

Many individuals, particularly in Asian nations, use astrological experts and charts to aid them in their quest to find the ideal companion. When seeking advice from astrologers, one of the most frequent questions eager people have is if they will find true love or their ideal mate. moreover, if their present partner is the ideal one for them. People believe that a perfect companion would be able to cover up all of their flaws.

Additionally, there are certain specialists who profit greatly from these destinists. With the aid of your DNA samples and plenty of money, they promise to provide you the opportunity to meet the ideal companion. It would be worthwhile to give these activities a try if you think they might bring real pleasure and complete harmony into your life.

We frequently ponder if love can be controlled into following a pattern when individuals believe that choosing the appropriate mate is the product of a meticulous and astrological approach. It might be difficult to decide to spend your whole life with someone who is nothing more than a well thought-out outcome of your star sign. Love is a natural phenomenon, and you can feel in your heart if someone is the right match for you or not. When two individuals sincerely love one other, compatibility is highly likely. You don't need an astrologer's assistance to determine if your companion is a sincere individual.

Simply because your stars align, you cannot wed someone you do not adore. According to traditional interpretations, planets in pleasant components provide favorable compatibility signals. Astrology makes an effort to compare facts strongly and produces predictions depending on the information given. Knowing each other's star signs makes you more informed and aware of one another. Religious convictions shouldn't hinder your ability to fall in love; rather, they should help you become a better person.

But the fundamental truth is that love recognizes no religion or star rating; it just develops between two people who then spend time together.

EXACTLY WHAT GUYS WANT IN A PARTNER

Women are more forthright about their needs and desires, but men's desires in relationships are sometimes a mystery. Men and women have distinct ways of thinking and acting, as well as different goals for relationships. Males reveal less than females, who make more efforts to communicate. Because they are unsure of what their husbands like or dislike, ladies find it difficult to make an impression on them. Don't worry, however. You have this chapter's support. I've explained what males want in a relationship in this chapter, along with what you can do to make it happen. What are you still holding out for? Let's get started.

Knowing what men want in a mate may help you to comprehend your spouse and show empathy for his unstated needs and desires. This could strengthen your bond and bring you closer together. It could also help you dispel myths and reduce any misunderstandings. So, what do men want in a partner? Let's investigate:

1. Men Desire Transparency in Relationships

For the majority of males, being honest comes first. Guys want to be able to trust their partners in committed relationships. Additionally, they want the trust be honored. A man cannot tolerate his wife keeping him in the dark about any matter. Despite how difficult it could be, they want to know the truth.

Steps to Take

Be straightforward in your communication. If your partner has shown trustworthy when you were dating and you two communicate openly about your desires and feelings, you should trust them. In every new dating relationship, it is inevitable for the partner who struggles with trust to take ownership of their worries when they arise. Otherwise, this behavior could eventually strain or damage a relationship.

2. Men don't like being in control in relationships

No man wants his wife to control or dominate him. Women often think they can change a man, but in order to have a strong, interdependent relationship with him, you must give him the freedom to spend time with his friends and pursue his interests. Some people can believe that they can manipulate a man into doing things. This is especially true if one of the spouses has a codependency. When a man's freedom and individuality are restricted or when he feels like he is being mothered, emasculated, and told what to do, this often has the opposite effect. This behavior typically turns a man off and isn't good for the longevity of a relationship.

Steps to Take

Define your boundaries and be honest with your partner. It's also essential to be open about what you want and expect from him. Keep in mind that it is not your partner's job to make you happy. It is your duty to do it.

3. Men Want Secure And Confident Partners

Men like women who are self-assured and conscious of the needs of their relationship partner. No matter if they are their friends, family, colleagues, or casual acquaintances, they do not want insecure partners and cannot stand to see them with other women. Any partner would feel cared for if a man is a great communicator with a partner and readily shares his objectives, such as where he is going and where they ended up going. Knowing that her lover is seeing another woman may make a lady feel insecure. However, if he is open and talks about his plans both before and after the event, he would start to build a far stronger connection for trust to grow—which is the most important cornerstone of any healthy relationship.

Steps to Take

Suspicion often results from insecurity, which may cause a lot of problems in a relationship. Have faith in your partner and the union as a whole. Take the time to learn about your behaviors and what happens when your trust button is pressed if you have trust issues. If you have a deep-seated belief that "all men are dishonest," even if a man is open and honest with you, you risk harming your relationship, future, and happiness.

4. Males Desire Acceptance for Who They Are

Men want their wives to accept them for who they are. They reject being compared to anybody. They are happy to be in a relationship where they are not required to act a specific way or live up to unrealistic standards.

Steps to Take

Don't pass judgment. Never criticize him in front of other people. Give him constructive criticism instead in private.

5. Men Want Dedication And Faithfulness

It is a common misconception that men constantly seek out relationships with several women. That is not always the case, however. A man can and will stay committed when he decides to become sincerely connected, and he expects the same behavior from his partner.

Steps to Take

Just being devoted is insufficient. Tell him how much the relationship matters to you in both your words and actions.

Men Desire Clearly Communicated With

A lack of open communication is the one thing that men do not want in a relationship. Guys really want you to express your sentiments and expectations in a relationship. You run the risk of creating misunderstanding if you put off sending a clear message.

Steps to Take

Every connection is built on communication. Maintain open lines of communication, be truthful when expressing your opinions and thoughts, and allow others to understand your thought process even when they disagree with you. It is advantageous to have a variety of thoughts. However, the best way to resolve a dispute is the one you choose.

Men Desire Respect 7.

One thing that men value much is respect. Your relationship can suffer if you insult him in front of others or keep your distance from him in private. Women who appreciate their husbands as well as their goals and aspirations are admired by men.

Steps to Take

Recognize and respect your boyfriend for who he is as well as his beautiful qualities. Instead of insulting him, express your displeasure with what you do not like about him.

8. Men Want Stability And Development

It's a common misconception regarding men that they don't value continuity or advancement in their relationships. However, the truth is that men want to get married to a responsible, mature partner.

Steps to Take

Be a mature person in your behavior. You'll be surprised at how quickly he'll want to advance the relationship if you provide a healthy environment for growth and maturity.

9. Men Want Emotional Closeness

The majority of men have been socialized to believe they cannot show signs of weakness or vulnerability. Such vulnerability entails expressing anxiety, displaying pain, exposing worries, etc. But some males do look to their relationship for emotional support. If they are made this way, they want a relationship where they can confide in their partner and feel comfortable sharing their fears, concerns, and feelings. When they are older, they will be more willing to express themselves if they were encouraged to do so when they were younger. A man will expose himself whenever he feels confident enough in you to do it on his own initiative.

Steps to Take

Be the emotional soundboard for him. Continue to reassure him that you are there to gently listen to all of his difficulties. When you accept him for how he shares and responds to an emotional connection with you, your relationship will become stronger. Since a woman's communication section of the brain is more developed than a man's emotional expression, he could not communicate his feelings as easily as a woman would. Without forcing him, give him space to express himself when he's ready.

10. Men want solitude in relationships. Even if he is completely committed to a woman, a man may still want to spend some time alone with her. He could prefer to be around his friends or sometimes need some time to himself to gather his thoughts.

Steps to Take

Distance is what a man needs in a relationship. Too much proximity often results in suffocation. Give the relationship with your partner some breathing room. Separate time alone is beneficial.

11. Men want a feeling of physical intimacy
Physical proximity and contact are essential in a relationship for men. He uses it to feel more intimately linked to you. However, just because there is a physical attraction does not mean he

wants to have sex with you all the time. It might be as simple as a hug, holding hands, or an ardent kiss.

Steps to Take

Men and women will have different needs in a relationship. Males like making connections via physical contact, whilst females adore communicating and sharing their worlds through words. To get to know him better and express what's important to you, ask him about the things that make him feel valued. For instance, when he spends quality time with you alone, when he listens to you, when he helps you, or when he compliments you and you feel appreciated and cherished. Just share the little acts of consideration you have shown for others.

12. Males Seek Security

In a relationship, security is something that both men and women need. A man will begin to consider you for a potential long-term commitment when he can still be himself, live independently from his relationship without feeling controlled, and you both communicate honestly. His confidence is boosted by his friends and activities. Additionally, he will be more motivated to commit himself if he knows that you are satisfied in your flesh. Being self-assured as an individual and as a couple results in a stronger, more secure, and devoted relationship that leads you both to the commitment that is right for you both.

Steps to Take

Tell your partner that for your relationship to last in the long run, developing a strong connection in the beginning is essential to you and that you have faith in him. This will reassure him that you respect his needs, his privacy, and the fact that building a stronger, more solid connection before you both commit to a long-term relationship requires honesty.

Men Expect To Be Comprehended, 13

After all, men are people too. They want their spouses to be understanding and not create a deal out of whatever mistakes they make. They desire to be accepted and encouraged despite their flaws.

Steps to Take

Anyone may make mistakes, even you. If he has messed up in any way, just let him know that it is okay. Make sure to let him know if the mistake has hurt you in any way, but also that you are willing to talk to him about it.

Men Want To Have Fun, 14.
Not only women find humor in their spouses to be endearing. Even men want it. They can unwind and relax when they have a fun-loving partner who doesn't take themselves too seriously. They want a friend that can be spontaneous, laugh along with them, and be willing to show off their playful side for this reason.

Steps to Take

Try to have some fun and be a bit playful. Watch your relationship strengthen as you both laugh at silly things.

15. Men Seek Connection Through Similar Interests

When their wives express interest in their hobbies and passions, men cherish it. Anything might be the cause, such as their passion for photography, playing the guitar, jogging, or another activity. It's a way for them to spend more time with you while still being content and enjoying themselves.

Steps to Take

Pay attention to what he does. If you have any queries, he will be happy to answer them and/or extend an invitation. If you make an effort to understand what matters to him, he will respect and share what matters to you.

16. Men Want Their Partner to Be Maturate

Every partnership has its fair share of conflicts. But if you don't reel it in once in a while, he can find the constant fighting annoying. Most men want their wives to handle challenges with maturity and clarity. Take note of your responses and actions. To see yourself from his point of view, put yourself in his position. Do you continue? Or do you respond responsibly?

Steps to Take

Instead of arguing about the issue or attempting to place the responsibility on him, avoid damaging arguments and make an effort to find a solution. Accept accountability for your emotions. Recognize your rage, take a moment to collect your emotions, and then decide when to respond.

Men Expect To Be Pampering 17.
Women are not the only ones that want some pampering in their relationships.

Men valued fair treatment. Even while they may not anticipate receiving flowers or chocolates every day, they will much enjoy receiving the occasional love note, a surprise gift, or a surprise date night.

Steps to Take

sometimes spoil him without any specific reason. Make him feel special by engaging in appealing and passionate behavior.

18. Men anticipate their partners to defend them.
Men are built to fight their battles by themselves. These difficulties might include coping with a financial calamity or battling with bad personal relationships. People want you to be on their side and help them, no matter what the challenge. They want you to defend them, to be their pillar of support, and to listen to them.

Steps to Take

Be at his side and firmly hold his hand. Inform him that you are there to support him and to talk with him about any challenges he wants to discuss. You don't need to stand up for him. His confidence will be increased just by your showing up and letting him know you are there for him.

19. Men Wish To Be Cared For

Simple acts of kindness go a long way toward strengthening ties and creating unshakable bonds. If you greet him with a smile and a warm hug after a long, stressful day, it will usually be enough to make him feel at ease. He will be happy to be with you. Put yourself in his shoes and give him some time to unwind before you talk about your day. To demonstrate that you are attentive to his needs, read his mood.

Steps to Take

Simply be there for him, greet him, and show him all your undivided love and care. He will then pick up on your good nature and learn to return the favor when you need anything done for you. Men are not as observant or as good at reading minds as women are. So be sure to let him know when you need a hug or a sympathetic ear.

Men like to feel important, number 20. In a relationship, men do not want to be taken for granted. They want to be a priority for the person they love, to be cherished and appreciated. Being inconsiderate to your partner's need for this might end your relationship. Let him know he is not alone when you show empathy for him. Inform him of your admiration for him or your regret for his difficult day. If you are unable to put his needs first, tell him right away that you will do so as soon as you can.

Steps to Take

Show him your concern. Even little acts of kindness, such as preparing his favorite meal after a bad day, or putting on his favorite music or TV show, may make him feel loved and cheered up.

Men Want Partnerships, Number 21
When their true love becomes a complete partner, men like that. They don't want her to remain as just a wife or girlfriend. They like it when their partner acts as a true friend, allowing them to confide and let their guard down.

Steps to Take

Turn becomes his confidant, companion, and buddy. Make an effort to fill that gap in his life where he feels incomplete.

Men may not express themselves as often as they should, but in a relationship, everyone wants to be seen, heard, and respected. Despite putting on a harsh front to conform to social expectations, males have similar relationship goals as women. Women may lack some emotional intelligence as a result of their socialization, but they may compensate by using their intuition and better communication skills. When you communicate your likes, dislikes, and expectations clearly, men adore you. They appreciate it when you take the relationship seriously but yet knowing how to have a good time and joke about with them. Never be afraid to spoil men; even if they don't say it outright, they like it when you sometimes care about them. We're sure you'll impress your partner with these fresh strategies in your toolbox!

Frequently Asked Questions: What influences a man's decision to trust a woman?

Men often believe that women are enigmatic and that they don't mean what they say. People thus see women as more trustworthy when they back up their claims with suitable conduct.

What emotional requirements does a guy have?

Despite their lack of emotional expression, men nevertheless have needs. They look to their partners for cozy company, affection, emotional stability, appreciation, and support.

Main Points
Men may or may not express their preferences and expectations, but most of the time, it's the little things that add up.
They may open up and express their deepest wants or anxieties with the support of clear communication, respect, and honesty.
Giving them their personal space is crucial in furthering the connection and communication, in addition to paying attention to their nonverbal clues and signs.
That is your duty to manage, not his. Take care of your happiness and well-being. Whether you're with him or not, he will admire you for your self-assurance and confidence.

WHERE TO LOOK ONLINE FOR YOUR SOULMATE

What Online Attracts Men?

You'll need some advice on online dating for women if you want to be effective at dating. It all depends on how you come across. Men rely their decision to ask you out on what you present in the first place. Men are undoubtedly quite visual, therefore having a nice picture can undoubtedly make a lady stand out online. What do they really search for, however, except the image?

They want advertisements that are truthful. Men want reassurance that they will find what they are seeking for. You should thus showcase who you are rather than what you believe men would find attractive. Make an effort to make your profile reflect the person they will meet on the first date if you're seeking for a serious partner. Instead of pretending to be someone you are not, try this instead.

Men want to converse with someone they believe to be genuine, therefore it's important to portray yourself as if you are conversing rather of just listing your qualifications and accomplishments as if you were presenting a CV. Make sure to include your favorite physical activities in your profile since people want someone they can do things with. When a guy sees that you share interests, he will be inspired to write since he can already see the two of you pursuing your passions together!

Men do not appreciate seeing insecurity in a woman. Remember that they may detect your neediness from a distance. Therefore, you had best take action if you believe that you lack self-confidence or self-esteem. But instead of writing about it, concentrate on the things you are confident in, like your job or your sense of style. Confidence is attractive to guys!

Men look for values in women as well. When the topic of religion or family is brought up, many women tend to withdraw out of concern that they will come out as too serious and turn men away. That is untrue! Many guys share your beliefs, and they will react when you explain what is most important to you!

If you keep the following tips in mind while creating your profile, you will undoubtedly get a lot of interest from men who might end up becoming your possible dates.

THE BEST WAYS TO MAKE AN ONLINE PROFILE

It's crucial that I restate something from the last chapter at the beginning of this one, in my opinion. Avoid giving out publicly accessible details like your phone number or address when creating dating profiles. Be aware that there are alternative applications that will enable you to connect with them as rapidly as text without disclosing a private number if the other party ever requests your phone number and you don't feel comfortable giving it to them. These include the cost-free Viber, Kik, and even Instagram. Provide your details if you are at ease doing so. If not, be cautious and meet in a place where you might even have a reliable buddy sit next to you without the other person knowing.

Creating a profile on the website of your choice is a crucial first step. In order to create a good profile, websites often include advice such, "Tell others what your hobbies and interests are," or "Describe what you look for in a partner." Take these actions. You wouldn't attend a job interview without a CV, and the same rule applies when creating an account on a dating website. Nothing is more demoralizing than seeing a beautiful set of images and a clever slogan lead to a profile where the about me section just states, "Ask me." I always shudder when this occurs. What do you want to know? What if you're a football fan but despise dogs? What would be the point of talking to you?

Actually, I wish a filtering option existed to exclude profiles without descriptions, similar to the one that eliminates profiles without photographs.

Make a new list if you have social anxiety or find it difficult to speak about yourself. Write down your strengths, your passions, your favorite authors, films, TV series, meals, and hangout areas. Tell your possible soul mate who you are; you already know who you are. Also, don't be hesitant to embrace and discuss the crucial traits you noted in Chapter Two. Describe how important your Presbyterian religion is to your daily life. On the other hand, be upfront if you happen to be Presbyterian and you sometimes attend services on certain holidays. Politics and a person's choice for a dog or cat are both examples of this. Another suggestion if you're still having trouble with your profile is to include a trusted buddy who is familiar with you. You might talk to your buddy about the types of things you want to include and then have them write a description on their own or work on one together.

The bulk of your profile is its description, but after that, give profile photo selection some thought. Consider the impression that you want to leave. Are you preppy, eccentric, geeky, or artistic? Even though they are all stereotypes, these are only a few instances. Choose the images that best represent you. Never, however, choose solely selfies or only group photos. If it's difficult for a possible match to identify you in a group photo, it might be annoying. One or two selfies indicate confidence, but just using selfies looks to reflect vanity. The best is diversity. Choose a couple that include you having fun with friends, one in which you are engaged in an activity you like, a picture of you, or even a selfie that captures your face in excellent detail. Choose photographs that are of decent quality but not exceptional quality. Too many flawless studio photographs may make your profile seem false for some mysterious psychological reason. However, if all of your images are blurry and were shot in dimly lit areas, they could not provide a good first impression. Also keep in mind that being a little bit seductive is OK, whether you're a male or a lady, but don't go overboard. If you're really looking for your soul mate, you don't want to take the chance of coming off as untrustworthy. Personal experience has shown me that refraining from posting obviously pornographic images has reduced the amount of obnoxious and pointless responses I get. But there's nothing wrong with a little sexiness, and I believe beach photos are typically OK. Take notice, guys: shirtless photos on a boat are far more attractive than mirror selfies of your abs.

Choosing your primary thumbnail image, tagline, and filters is the last step. A thumbnail photo that is close up on your face and effectively highlights your attributes is something I would definitely recommend. A wise decision is always to smile. Make sure your slogan is clever, catchy, or intriguing when choosing one. Instead of simply saying "Hi" or "Get at Me," try starting your message with one of your favorite jokes or a quote from a significant work of literature or cinema. This will pique people's attention and make them more inclined to visit your profile. Once you've customized every aspect of your profile, establish filters to allow just the matches you want to hear from. From site to site, filters may vary, but they will often contain things like gender, age range, geographical range, height, body type, and purpose.

The exciting part is about to begin: meeting possible soul mates!

In Chapter 4,

The ability to cope with anything comes from knowledge. You may be startled to learn that you often speak to yourself in a manner that you wouldn't typically speak to most other people. Keep a small journal to help you become more conscious of how you speak to yourself. Label one side of the sheet as positive and the other as negative after drawing a line down the center of it. Record your self-talk throughout the day, from dawn to night, or even for a whole week. Include all of your thoughts, even the brief ones that you had a moment ago but didn't signify a thing.

By rating oneself, you might also become more conscious of how much you value yourself. How would you rate your level of self-love, from 1 to 100? One indicates that you don't love yourself, and one hundred indicates that you do.

The first step is to understand where you are with yourself. Taking action is the last step in fostering self-love in your life. Positive affirmation should come first. You may start loving yourself in a variety of ways.

Start by composing a letter to yourself. Write a letter to your younger self in the voice of your present self. What would you want to say to yourself? What advice would you give to yourself when you were younger? The past cannot be altered, so keep that in mind. You are already aware of what this youngster will experience. How would you assist them get through it in your writing?

Another option is to compose a letter in the role of an understanding and caring friend. How does your buddy support you when you share your troubles with them? What advice do your friends provide when you reveal your hopes for love? What advice does your sympathetic and kind buddy provide when you share your objectives and dreams? Keep this letter close at hand. And pull out the letter and read it whenever you feel overtaken by events, people, or your emotions. Remind yourself that you are the one who does care.

Writing a letter to your future self is yet another technique to get your ideas on self-love. Tell your future self in a letter how you arrived to their current state of happiness, love, and freedom. Describe how you are taking better care of yourself. Give whatever advice you have and the lessons you've learnt to your future self. and keep it. Put it aside and read what you wrote to yourself again after a year, two years, or three years. Read the letter you wrote to yourself with love, care, and concern.

Stretching in the morning, evening, or while you're in the shower are other everyday self-love exercises that you may do. Creating a mantra you may repeat daily and as often as required during the day is one way to improve your self-love. Your own mantra may be created. It simply has to be truthful, positive, and about you. Even if these mantras are true from the first day you employ them, it will take some time for you to start believing them when you repeat them regularly or when you are in need. For instance: I'm worth it.

I'm doing it because I can.

Here are a few more:

I am significant. I am worth my own time, in other words.

I am competent. I don't have to improve to be good enough, therefore. Where I am, I adore it.

I simply need my own approval. I don't have to make concessions to appease others, in other words.

The way others treat me is a reflection of them, not of me. I don't ask to be treated badly, in other words. Even by myself, I do not deserve to be treated badly.

I will observe before I act, which means that before I make a snap choice, I will evaluate the situation and the involved parties to choose the best course of action.

I'll reply rather than react. - I'll take the time to think things through carefully and come to a choice I'm proud of.

A stepping stone, that is. - I'm laying the groundwork for my future self. My current actions will assist me in achieving my objectives.

My objectives are attainable. This means that I can attempt new things and take calculated risks. Failure is not the finish; rather, it is the start. I can manage it.

I adore myself.

I have faith. I am skilled or talented, in other words. I'm helpful.

I trust in myself. In other words, I CAN!

Because you are writing and reciting these mantras in your own handwriting and voice, you will find it easier to accept them. When the heart hears the truth, it recognizes it. However, there are occasions when your own thoughts and speech deceive you.

Self-doubt is a bully that is essentially imperceptible. It begins with pointing out all of your transgressions and concludes by telling you that you are unworthy of anything and that you shouldn't even bother trying. This is a falsehood since negative self-talk will not recognise all of your accomplishments. It ignores the advancement you have previously achieved and refuses to accept the actions you are now doing to better yourself and your life.

Positive affirmation may be used to counter negative self-talk. Make a list of all your good traits. Ask some of your friends if they can think of any of your strengths. If it makes you uncomfortable, establish a list of desirable attributes. These may be written on sticky notes and placed on your bathroom mirror or another location where you will be sure to see them every day at sunrise. One may even be placed in your vehicle, wallet, or other inventive places.

Commence in the morning or as soon as you awaken. Say out loud, "I am..." and then identify the characteristic when you look at the attributes on the sticky note. For each sticky note, say this loudly. Say it loudly and with sincerity. And when you speak with them, do your best to uphold that standard. After all, our perception of our worth is based on both our abilities and, more crucially, our actions. Use "to the best of your ability" as a yardstick for what you can do if you want to maximize the impact of your talents in the actual world. It's a terrific idea to do this practice to rewire the way you hear yourself talking about yourself. Even if you have doubts, you'll ultimately notice a shift in your self-talk.

Self-care is a vital component of self-love. It makes sense to spend money on a good pair of shoes or in-soles to assist protect your feet if you spend the most of the day on your feet. Self-love includes ensuring that your body receives appropriate nutrition, rest, and relaxation.

You are abusing yourself if the majority of your diet is unhealthy. You are ignoring yourself if you put off seeing the doctor for any medical problem. You are abusing yourself if you are not taking care of your necessities or if you are living in squalor. You are abusing yourself if you starve yourself to reduce weight and become in shape.

Additionally, if you are mistreating yourself, you are letting undesirable traits and bad energy into your life.

Think about whether you keep your home organized and clutter-free. It is well recognized that a tension undercurrent in the house is rooted in clutter. It prevents creativity and overpowers your senses of touch, smell, and vision. Clutter makes it harder to relax mentally and physically and signals to your brain that you still have work to do, in addition to the unpleasant sensations that come with having a dirty home. Doing things for oneself is a component of self-love and positive affirmation, and cleaning for oneself is one of those things. They could drop over unexpectedly at any time, but it's not for your business. Small adjustments may be made around the home until a healthy habit is formed.

Make your bed when you get up in the morning before leaving the room. Teach yourself to do the dishes before going to bed. Make yourself put five items in their proper places before leaving your desk, sofa, or chair. You'll be able to tell the difference in how you feel about living in that atmosphere after you stop doing these activities after doing them consistently for a while. Because you are taking care of yourself to demonstrate that you value yourself and are worth your own efforts, this supports your positive affirmations. It's worthwhile to invest in you!

THE RELATIONSHIPS AND THE LAW OF ATTRACTION

According to some, the Law of Attraction may work in the areas of money, health, and happiness. Living a happy life includes having satisfying connections. These might be friendships, family bonds, or passionate love relationships. They are all impacted by the Law of Attraction.

The Law of Attraction is constantly at work, whether or not you are attempting to employ it in your life. You are always releasing vibrations into the cosmos. They continually gather with other people who have comparable energy and return to you. So, smile and enjoy yourself. Everyone finds happiness attractive. Nobody likes to be around those who are always down or whining. If you are having trouble finding reasons to be joyful, consider keeping a gratitude journal. Every day, record something for which you are thankful in this diary. Start with the first few that come to mind. Start with having access to oxygen to breathe, waking up in the morning, being able to see, hear, touch, etc. if you are having trouble thinking of anything. You'll soon come to the realization that you have a lot to be grateful for. When you stop to think about it, we all have a lot to be grateful for. Read this diary if you're feeling down.

When you consciously use the Law of Attraction, there is a difference because your attention is on the things you desire. These good things then come back to you. Your life revolves around the things you pay attention to.

You will get excited about something once it becomes significant to you. A power bigger than any you can summon by just repeating words about what you desire will emerge from that exhilaration. Just as it does in everything else, the Law of Attraction also applies to relationships.

You may locate the one you're seeking for by consciously using the Law of Attraction. The first stage is to decide what you want from a partner. List everything. Make a list of the qualities you want the individual to possess. Jot down any delights you want to share. You must first select what qualities you need in a soulmate before setting out to acquire them all for yourself. You must be athletic yourself if you desire someone who is. Examine each quality on your list, then start making progress toward achieving it.

The universe will use the Law of Attraction to bring you to your partner after you have a clearer sense of what you desire. Through the matching of frequencies, this will occur. You broadcast the desired frequency. This vibration spreads and gathers with other similar frequencies.

It is just a question of time until you meet someone when your frequency is vibrating in unison with another frequency. It will be the Law of Attraction in action. You should now rely on your intuition. accomplish it if the need strikes you to accomplish something on a different timetable than normal. You could discover your soul partner in this way.

Simply let the Law of Attraction to operate. Keep telling yourself that you can find the person you're seeking for. Have faith that you will locate that someone. Bring the topic to your attention and arouse your interest. There will be events.

The Law of Attraction will give you a partner in despair if you are depressed. You will both be better off if you choose to use the Law of Attraction to your advantage rather than against you as the two of you descend. Look for methods to make your frequencies resonate harmoniously and favorably. Like nothing else, this will make relationships stronger and last longer.

Your connections may grow into something greater than they have ever been. Friendships with people may get deeper. You and your family members can coexist peacefully. Your romantic interests may end up becoming mates for life. The Law of Attraction has the power to manifest anything.

How to Make Communication Better

Take time for you and your partner, for example, as one of the things you would wish to accomplish. Try going for a stroll while conversing about the weather or other stress-relieving subjects. Until you're prepared to talk about your concerns calmly, you should steer clear of stressful topics. Calling the shots while emotions are high is among the greatest errors individuals make. This results in a screaming fight where nobody prevails.

You can regulate your emotions and learn to relax if you can speak without taking offense. After spending some time together just conversing, you may feel like spending a romantic evening together.

In order for a connection to flourish, two people are required. Noting is simple. Every partnership has challenging moments. Think only on your partner's positive traits. Tell them how much you value what they accomplish well. Be precise. Tell your partner if they have strong listening abilities. Tell your partner about all your mutual qualities. Keep in mind that what you concentrate on growing. The only person you should think about if you are considering all your negative characteristics is yourself. Improve your personal life by working hard. Nobody is changeable. You can only improve your life by working on yourself. If you make changes in your life, your partner can become interested in you and begin making changes in their relationship. It has been shown that actions speak louder than words.

But when you learn to communicate, you lay the foundation for a brighter future. One of the main causes of failed relationships is a lack of communication. Various methods of communication exist. Sometimes learning occurs best when you sit and listen while also observing gestures or body language. The secret to success and learning how to acquire abilities that help you enhance your own life is observation.

Values for a Better Personal Life

Our personal values determine how we spend our time, energy, and money. When our principles are strong, we may go as far as we can in terms of enhancing our personal lives. We make choices about how we want to spend our time throughout our lives. Time is of the essence since it passes quickly.

The typical individual works for the majority of the day. After work, people go home to spend time with their spouse and family, watching television, or participating in activities. Making time for yourself is equally crucial. Everyone needs some time alone.

It requires action to make life better. The first step in making a change is to sit down, develop a list, establish a strategy, and set objectives. Take it easy on yourself. Since positive thinking is the secret to success, look at the good instead of all the negative. One project at a time. Once your objectives are established, start acting to enhance your personal life. Learn something new, enroll in a course, experiment with a new workout, pick up a new sport, visit new locations, etc. Any part of your life may be improved, including your physical, spiritual, mental, emotional, etc. state. Once again, your partner could show interest and decide to work with you to improve your life as a couple.

YOU AS WELL ENJOY MUSICAL THEATER?

I've been active with musical theater since I was a small child. I began when I was ten years old, and during my adolescence I appeared in several musicals. I had a couple crushes on men each performance, but I never went after them since I was still a kid and didn't really know what flirting really meant. It was no surprise that all the guys I had crushes on turned out to be homosexual as I grew older and understood that musical theater only draws a small number of heterosexual males.

In high school, I had a serious infatuation on a musical theater actor, but during that time, he had a girlfriend. She was not at all appealing, but he was adorable. A few years later, I watched him making out with his new lover and realized that I had never understood why he was dating her in the first place. I swore I would never be a woman in a committed relationship with a guy who is questioning his sexual orientation.

I simply want to emphasize that I'm LGBTQ-friendly before I go on. One of the best colleges in the nation for LGBTQ acceptance is Ithaca College, which I attended. I have many friends in each of those groups, and I have also trained many individuals in each of those categories. I've come to terms with the fact that my passion in theater tends to draw mostly homosexual males to the stage.

But I want the guys I date to be categorically heterosexual. That isn't a really high bar, in my opinion. And since I was around by many homosexual guys while I was growing up, I developed a quite accurate "gaydar." A whopping 4 percent of respondents say they identify as LGBTQ, and it's likely that many more either don't say or aren't sure yet. In other words, there's a possibility that if I go on 20 dates with 20 different men, one of them will be homosexual or question his sexual orientation.

For some reason, even on first dates, males seem truly at ease telling me about their lives. They continue sharing secrets when they see my unjudgemental countenance since I've heard so many bizarre things that nothing surprises me anymore. Amazingly, males have admitted to fantasizing about guys, finding men more appealing than women, or sometimes engaging in same-sex activities.

confined to a closet

When he revealed to his parents that he was homosexual, one of the men I dated said they sent him to treatment for five years in order to "get the gay out." I was the first woman he went on a date with, but shortly after, he came out as homosexual.

Another man I went out with said that his mother was the sole living member of his family. He dated women to appease her since she wanted him to have children so badly. He exhibited no interest in me, but his eyes brightened up and his pace picked up as soon as we passed a male buddy of his. I felt like the third date on my own date as they excessively flirted with each other in front of me. Undoubtedly, a romantic connection was forged that day, but not with me.

I was saddened by these folks. They led lives in denial of the reality. They lied about who they were and who they wanted to be with in order to get the approval of their parents and friends. I wanted to assist them, but it wasn't my position to do so. The coach in me wanted to. Since it was obvious to both of us that we were seeking different—or, technically, the same—things, I was unable to date them any longer. We both desired males. They just lacked the self-assurance to tell themselves and the rest of the world that.

Does going to an expensive restaurant mean you're getting engaged?

Michael and my friend Amanda dated for a while, and Amanda believed he would soon pop the question. She informed me she had met her soul mate and was madly in love with him. I was very happy for her when she contacted me one day and said, "This is going to be the night!" She was aware that Michael was going to ask her to be his wife since he was bringing her to a luxury restaurant.

While I waited eagerly by the phone, Amanda started sobbing and mumbled words I couldn't make out. My stomach fell as her words finally made sense. He made no proposal. He no longer want to date her. He really had lost interest in dating women. He aspired to female gender. He felt the urge to tell her the news at a fine dining establishment. He had gender confirmation surgery to become the lady he had always desired after they split up.

My main point was that although I felt dreadful for Amanda, I also felt bad for Michael (who later changed his name to Michelle). Fortunately, Michelle ultimately accepted her reality before marrying someone to whom she no longer had sexual attraction. She had been trapped in the incorrect gender for a very long time. If they had been married before Michelle told Amanda and herself that she was engaged, things would have been much more difficult. Even though it was a terrible period for them both, they eventually had the freedom to live their own lives and find the companions they want.

Summary If you are certain that you are straight, you should confirm that the man you are dating is likewise straight. You'll always be concerned that he may leave you for a male if he exhibits signs of sexual ambiguity.

Total Respect For The Other Person

Both sides must have the utmost regard for their other in order for a relationship to go the distance. When you don't respect someone you are in a relationship with, that connection rapidly deteriorates.

Being entirely honest with one another and holding your spouse in extremely high regard are examples of having respect for one another. You HAVE to let your spouse know if you believe they have lied or if they continue to act in a way that erodes your respect for them. You must have the courage to tell them that their actions make you respect them less, and you don't want that to happen. They will cease doing such things if your relationship is solid and they respect you, which will increase your mutual regard. Speaking out will earn you their respect, and you'll regard them much more for being considerate of your sentiments.

If you remain silent and your spouse continues to act in a way that makes you lose respect for them, it will eventually turn into animosity. Make careful to speak out when issues are minor to avoid them growing into animosity. Perhaps you are not meant to be together if they won't respect your preferences, even if they are reasonable ones.

Now complete the task on the next page. Download the workbook for FREE here.

Action Step 10: Complete Respect for Everyone

Your spouse should be someone you: Respect, are proud of, and will defend.

Place complete faith in

Your partner is the person you are in a relationship with, whether you are dating or married. With adequate respect for one another, it should be a very solid tie that cannot be broken.

What further methods are there to convey your undying admiration for your partner?

Aligned Values and Goals, Step 11

This is crucial for a happy relationship to have. Goals may be modified at any moment, but your life is guided by your values, which are more significant. Your relationship will suffer greatly if your values are out of sync, and either you or your spouse risk losing respect for the other.

When individuals are dating, this is one topic that they often avoid discussing. Religion, table etiquette, work ethic, child rearing, child discipline, how we treat others, how we respect our elders, etc. are just a few examples of values. It won't work out if you truly feel that the only way to succeed in life is to work hard and think strategically while your spouse has no issue taking advantage of others to advance in life.

It is crucial that both sides raise the issues that are most important to them. There are two ways to get here. You will be far ahead of most couples if you can connect your deepest values. It is best to understand this in the outset so you can save yourself years of emotional suffering.

Although your individual goals and objectives may not be the same—in fact, they probably aren't—it is crucial that you are all traveling in the same direction. There has to be some compromise if one of your aims is to live on a tropical beach and the other's goal is to live in Alaska and go ice fishing every day. The fact that most couples have polar opposite preferences for heat is amusing. Typically, a lady prefers a warm home than a chilly one for the guy. Things of such kind are simple to resolve.

I'm thinking about more ambitious aims when I say this. Polar opposites in this area will lead to a lot of conflict. There will be opposition if one of you is content to host barbeques every weekend and play in a softball league while the other wants to take over the world. There are some couples who can work things out, but it is best if you and your partner have similar life objectives.

Now complete the task on the next page. Download the workbook for FREE here.

Step 11: Aligned Values and Objectives

Spend some time here identifying the values that are most important to you.

Step 12: Pay attention to what your partner needs and finds satisfying.

Every individual has six basic wants that must be met, which is one of the things I've learnt through my coaching training with Tony Robbins and Robbins Madanes Training. They are as follows:

the need for affection and intimacy. That seems pretty apparent, no? We all have this urge, which may be satisfied by a love partner, members of our family or friends, our pets, or even a group or gang. People will go against their own ideals and do everything else they can to satisfy their desires, whether it is good or evil.

the desire for clarity. Certainty is having the assurance that one will be cared for or that a loved one, such as a child's love, will be there for them. Certainty is the conviction that, despite working 70 hours a week, you will always be able to provide for your family and keep a roof over their heads. It is the knowledge that all of your fundamental needs are being addressed. Knowing beyond a shadow of a doubt that your spouse cares for you and will remain at your side no matter what.

the need for doubt. Additionally, we need ambiguity or diversity. There wouldn't be any thrill if every day was the same. Variety and surprise are essential. This may be done by giving yourself a thrill by riding a motorbike at top speed, skydiving, dressed sexily for your spouse, going on a date, or even initiating a fight, which would cause you to experience a range of emotions. Drugs and alcohol will also let you experience a range of emotions.

the need for importance. Everyone needs to believe that they matter or are relevant. They need a sense of significance. People will construct harmful means to get significance if they do not experience it positively, for as via violence or developing a disease that requires medical attention.

a need for expansion. For a person to really feel alive, they must advance and evolve. Some individuals will stop at nothing to satisfy this urge, but if they do not continue to develop, they will never be satisfied. What doesn't flourish perishes.

the need to provide more than oneself. This may include everything from helping the environment, our children, or someone else's life by teaching them anything. Again, individuals don't always seek this urge, but they need it to feel whole and satisfied.

Since each person in a relationship is so unique, it is crucial for us to understand what makes our spouse feel loved, significant, or certain as well as the kinds of ambiguity or variation they like. Do you two develop together and give back to others as a couple? By providing our spouse what these things mean to us, we cannot satisfy their wants. We must provide for them in their manner.

How many couples do you know whose wives like making their husband feel loved and special by doing unique things for him on important occasions? Since the husband dislikes receiving special treatment, he would by default refrain from providing it for his wife.

Here, communication is lacking. While the wife's generosity to her husband makes her feel wonderful, it does not make him feel wonderful. Because he is doing what comes naturally to him, he does not give to her in a manner that would make her feel special. The requirements of each party are not being met. Because, in her opinion, if she truly meant to him, he would do special things for her as well, she is left feeling undervalued and insignificant. Do you understand what I'm saying?

One may experience love in particular ways while the other may not. Our responsibility is to investigate or just inquire what makes our spouse feel unique, cherished, etc. Some of us like receiving things, others enjoy receiving acts of service, yet others enjoy being touched, and still others need nothing more than quality time. We need to know how to make our partners feel entirely pleased so that they would reciprocate in the manner we want if we want to have a wonderful, long-lasting relationship. Do you understand this?

Gary Chapman's book "The 5 Love Languages" is the one that best describes this. I strongly advise you to get this book. It clarifies how our individual major love languages differ. We won't feel loved if this essential love language is not acknowledged. They won't feel loved even if we offer our loved ones all the love we can in our own love language but not in theirs.

When reflecting on former relationships that didn't work out, consider the five love languages and the six basic human needs. Then, rate how well your partner and you both met those needs on a scale of 1 to 10. Look at these inquiries together.

How important do you think I made my spouse feel? Was it my kids, my family, my career, or my friends that felt they came first, or did they believe it was them?

How much love did I everyday infuse into my relationship? Was that how they envisaged love?

How certain were they that I would support them and ensure that we would have a roof over our heads?

How varied was the interaction between us? Were we having fun and having adventures every day, or was everything regular and my partner feeling like they needed to pursue excitement elsewhere?

Did your partnership improve as a result of your efforts to improve your lives or your relationship?

Did we help ourselves or others more?

This might enlighten you much as to the potential causes of the failure of previous relationships. People being unfaithful most often do so because their wants are not being addressed. This will open your eyes in a big way for your next relationship. One of the most crucial elements of both this book and life is this.

Asking yourself how you want your needs in these areas to be satisfied would be a terrific exercise for you to do, after which you could test your spouse with the results. Have you ever heard someone remark, "I wish they understood me?" Don't make them figure it out, by all costs. Let them in on all the information. We want them to succeed. They're hoping you succeed. No more speculating. Give them the exam answers. ;)

Now complete the task on the next page. Download the workbook for FREE here.

If you are currently dating someone, fill out this form for them; if not, consider a former lover. In this phase, you will: First, consider how you believe your spouse wishes to have their needs addressed; Second, describe how you would want to have your needs satisfied in the questions; Third, evaluate how well you and your spouse satisfy each other's requirements.

TO FIND SELF-LOVE, BE CLEAR.

You must learn to be CLEAR if you want to love yourself. In the quest for self-love, the meaning of the term clear becomes evident. Self-love demands self-assurance, admiration, regard, acceptance, and respect for oneself.

- To be confident, you must have confidence in yourself and have faith in your talents.
- To like someone, you must be content with and like who they are as a person.
- To feel self-empowered, you must value your own perspective and way of life.
- To be accepted, you need to accept and believe in who you are all the time.
- Respect demands that you pay great attention to how you feel and to your own needs. When you can reflect on your words, acts, and actions and know that you have performed properly and

with integrity, that is when you respect yourself.

Claim, Declare, Call Out, and Counsel all have a same origin. Currently, it means being "transparent, easily seen or heard, not obscure, open, obvious, certain" as well as "free from guilt, free from debt, free from obstruction, free from impurities, innocent."

You must be completely transparent when making a declaration or a claim. Speaking frankly and honestly about whatever you're feeling within, no matter what it is, implies that you're innocent by definition.

You won't be penalized for it as long as you are remaining true to the truth that you now hold in your heart of hearts (and that aligns with unselfish love rather than selfishness).

DO NO HARM is the one and only golden law of love. Treating all living things with respect is how you ensure that you do no damage.

You will find yourself, your partner, wealth, and genuine and lasting happiness by practicing being clear and uttering authentic words from the heart as heard with the inner ear.

The definition of "real" in the English language is "existing as or actually, true, genuine, authentic, honest, free from deceit." You can't play a character, wear a mask, or deceive if you want to be genuine.

The word "ear" derives from the verb "perception," which means "to take hold of, feel, comprehend, to grasp mentally, to recognize, observe, and to be aware of." Using your inner ear means paying attention to your heart's feelings, particularly what your conscience or gut instinct is trying to tell you.

In addition to being a necessary muscle, the heart is described as the "innermost feelings or passion." It is said to be the location of the soul, the self's guiding voice, which can only be heard inside.

The words "heart" and "courage" are etymologically related and may be used interchangeably. The Latin term anima, which means soul, is the source of the Romanian word inima, which means heart. Inner hearing is the knowledge of your heart's and soul's true emotions.

The expressions "heart-to-heart talk," "follow your heart," "listen to your heart," and "speak from the heart" are well known. Using your inner ear to hear what your heart or soul is saying and then acting on it is known as acting from the heart.

Instead of acting on the advice of the fear-based, animalistic ego, which is driven by the want to protect oneself at all costs, the objective is to follow the conscience's guidance of unselfish love.

You must have the guts to be REAL and to follow your conscience wherever it may go if you want to be CLEAR. Your higher-self, also known as your conscience, which gets guidance from the Holy Spirit, may be heard via your inner ear by paying attention to your sentiments and motives and comparing them to selfless love. This is how you communicate with your soul, the aspect of you that resides in the spirit world.

You must have the confidence to follow your gut and do what feels right for you because it is motivated by genuine love rather than selfishness. This will put you in alignment with Divine Love.

Your safety and prosperity are here. You will discover your soul partner, love for yourself, success, stability, and enduring happiness by being clear about your own reflection and by making selfless love the guiding principle of your moral code of behavior.

Before you say or act, pause and reflect on how you actually feel. Have the fortitude to be honest about what you learn after tuning in to the innermost impulses of your conscience. Always submit to the rule and service of the unfailing, unselfish Divine Love. You need to work on yourself if what you discover in your heart conflicts with this love.

Support pure love—Divine Love—in speech, action, and thought. No matter what you think the consequence could be, act in accordance with what your conscience tells you to do. You will be protected and supplied for in every manner as long as you are hearing and serving Divine Love, and you will find the tranquility that beyond all comprehension.

Every action you do must be motivated by selfless love and must not damage anybody. Because you receive back what you put out, they must be treating you how you would have wanted to be treated.

If you are being persuaded to injure any living thing—harm that you wouldn't want done to you—this is not the voice of your conscience. These desires stem from your ego's need to protect itself and are motivated by fear. They represent the animal or monstrous side of human nature, which is driven by the instinct for survival of the fittest and prioritizes the preservation of oneself above all others.

The battle for your conscience to choose whether you should behave from a position of unselfish love (Christ consciousness) or selfishness (Devil consciousness) is always raging inside of you, much as it is in cartoons, with an angel or a demon on each shoulder. Which one will you let triumph?

FIGURE 5

Sam and I had gotten so close that going out to eat without him would be agonizing. Sam and I hadn't begun seeing each other romantically until a month later.
He wanted to spend more time with me, was more present around me, and spoke with confidence. But he was respectful of my space and not at all hurried.

We made the decision to go slowly and not force anything in our relationship. It was odd because the man I thought was just an ordinary employee suddenly became someone I wanted to spend every day with.

We had lovely date evenings. We would plan exciting road trips or fun hitchhikes on the weekends. I started to become brave and adventurous; a side of myself I never knew existed came out to play.

He made me the center of his universe and made sure that I was completely informed of every choice he made so that I wouldn't be caught off guard. He understood me so well that I didn't need to utter a word before he knew what was on my mind since we spent so much time together. Communication between us was natural and uncomplicated. He turned into my rock, taught me to always have confidence in myself, reminded me of how gorgeous I am, and made it clear that he always wanted me by his side.

He had to be the one since he was compassionate, kind, patient, and self-assured, and because this time I had a whole different emotion and felt like time flew by while we were together. My feet were securely placed next to his, and I felt secure.

We treasured every hour we spent together, and the desire to never want to part was shared. We treated each other with such care and respect, understood what we wanted, and respected one other's limits.

Sam looked like a lovely man and would often check to see how I was doing both at work and outside of it. He also shared some basic information and opinions with me, and there was something I found particularly intriguing about him.

Same was adamant on starting a family, expanding it, and raising children.

At least it's worth a shot, he reasoned.

How I was able to make Sam fall in love with me beyond simply my attractive appearance was a mystery to me while we were together since it seemed like a brilliant light was just glowing over my head.

He let me know that I was enough for him now and always would be, and he hoped I felt the same way about him.

We would snuggle till I fell asleep in his arms. He prepared me delectable meals and brought them to me in bed. He would murmur in my ear, telling me how beautiful I looked every day and how confident I was.

I knew he was the one, it had to be him.

AVOID COMMON RELATIONSHIP BLUNDERS

The saying "human beings are prone to error" is ubiquitous, however it does not apply in all circumstances, and not all errors are preventable. When it comes to finding your soul partner, this is very true. A shattered heart is similar to a broken pot in that cracks will always be there no matter how hard you attempt to patch them up.

I recall that back then, I used to overindulge in slaying beauty queens. I met a beauty queen who certainly had all the attributes I was looking for in a soul mate if I had cared to inquire more, but I once said to her, "hey! How would you expect me to be stooping over you merely to listen to your whispers when you are just too short to hang over the edges of my shoulders? We were really in one of those jubilant and exuberant situations, but my beauty queen Cynthia went to her knees, cupped her face in her hands, and I could see tears trickling down the pits of her fingers. I knelt down, tried to comfort her, and expressed my regret in a variety of sorrowful ways, but nothing seemed to stick.

It took Cynthia around fifteen minutes to collect her composure and the confidence she needed to begin. We had a bad start to our relationship after that. The former Miss Universe quickly transformed into one of the coldest comforters to wrap yourself in. Our whole connection eventually became chilly, and despite my best efforts to keep it alive, it eventually withered away.

Yes, Cynthia is gone. I hurt her feelings. No matter how hard I tried, the fractures in her heart would not totally close. I will remember this lesson for the rest of my life.

I disregarded My Soul Mate Plan's most important rule: how not to be! I probably wouldn't have gone down that road with Cynthia if I had given this more thought. Additionally, I wouldn't have dated infertile people.

You don't have to make as foolish a mistake as I did to learn from it. I took the risk of trekking through the jungle, but fortunately the way is now clearer for you. Although I was scratched by the thorns of my errors, this book shows you the way clearly. Let me describe the thorns that did puncture my skin when I made the road through the bush; I refer to them as typical methods of HOW NOT

TO BE; sure, the 12 disciples should avoid them;

1. becoming very annoyed

Errors are made by people. You shouldn't become too irritated if the repeated error is being made despite your repeated cautions.

You already know how Cynthia stumbled when I said, "Hey! How would you expect me to be stooping over you merely to listen to your whispers when you are just too short to hang over the edges of my shoulders?It was such a huge error on my part. Even though she did show forgiveness and I did apologize again, I was also very hurt by her extreme irritability. To this day, however, I still feel regret.

She did tell me why she was unable to restrain herself after making multiple attempts at reconciliation. "You are not the first one, in fact, you are the third boyfriend who has had issues with my height," she said simply. "When I thought I had finally found the one who didn't mind my height, you just threw in a bombshell that ruptured every little faith I held onto that my height would no longer matter." Yes, uncontrollable annoyance seldom comes from a single incident. It is something that becomes more ingrained in your memory over time and is reinforced each time, much like a cattle track. I'm not saying you have to never get annoyed. There are irritations and they serve as useful indicators of things you should pay attention to, but how you handle them may create or break even the strongest of bonds.

2. being needlessly stupid

The biggest barrier to finding a soul mate is a lack of communication. Your soul mate wants and deserves to talk to you all the time. The finest way for him or her to communicate their inner spirit is via this. Your souls cannot be soul mates if he or she expresses their inner selves while you refuse to do the same with regard to your own inner selves.

I previously discussed the kind of criticisms I often heard from my beauty queens, including "Why do you like concealing secrets?", "Why do you hesitate to express your ideas to me?", "Why don't you introduce yourself to me more?". These concerns were a blatant example of my poor communication.

If you genuinely want to find your soul partner, communication is essential since it is the language that souls are most familiar with. Words are vital for your intellect, but the soul cares more about how they are presented than they do about the cleverness of the words that are said.

3. Having disagreements before bed

Being irritable before bed is the quickest way to end romance. You eliminate all potential dream sources, leaving only nightmares to be welcomed into the emptiness.

In a "come-we-stay" kind of relationship for a time, I squatted into marital territory with one of the beauty queens, and she was such a wonderful lady in bed. Her name was Rose. However, Rose's one flaw is that, while we are having typical pre-sexual rants, she will suddenly bring up a demand just as her thongs are about to come off. This would lead to several disagreements and discussions, the resolution of which would finally cause us to fall asleep tied back-to-back like Siamese twins.

I do not deny that every bed of roses has its thorns, but why wait until things have begun to steam up before adding some cold water? Because of this negative behavior, soul mates' sexual affinities suffer. Just because you have the key to the carnal gate doesn't mean you should keep your spouse captive! This can as well mean that your soul partner becomes an unwanted stranger. What else would you anticipate? It's the end of romance! Ever heard of soul mates that aren't in a relationship? That is a rare breed that is in danger of becoming extinct.

4. Possessive family members and friends controlling your connection

allow your soul partner be the first person you allow in when you decide to do so! There are some overly nosy and bothersome friends that prefer to snoop about in your affairs. If you allowed them in, an unpleasant odor would come from somewhere you didn't expect it.

The tallest beauty queen I've ever beaten was Daisy. Actually, she worked as a model. Her presence was so loud around me. A group of her male pals would pretentiously take turns guarding a hive whenever she came near me. I barely ever got the opportunity to talk to Daisy alone. Every time this group of guys surrounded me, I would pretentiously pretext that I was with some other 'boys' nearby while really quietly observing how the other lads were struggling to resist Daisy's alluring beauty. She was welcome to complain to me about how some of my friends were attempting to woo her. I didn't bother however since I was certain that none of them could charm her. Daisy, however, saw this as a sign that I didn't value, care for, or want Daisy.

Every soul partner sees themselves as important in your eyes and demands unrestricted room inside your realm. Yes, you are supposed to serve just your soul mate since, as the adage goes, "you can never serve two masters at the same time." I'm not suggesting you cut off links or ignore other relationships, but you shouldn't ignore your soul partner either!

It didn't take me long to see that my relationship with Daisy had begun to deteriorate. As egotistical as I was, I did make an effort to act unconcerned. I found myself asking, "How can she make me so weak to reject my male company? What would other guys think of me if I give in to a girl?Yes, my ego caused me to stumble in front of my fellow guys.

5. putting water on the romance's flames

The flames of romance must remain lit since it is the warmth that sustains the connection of soulmates. Love shouldn't be taken for granted. No spark will be left to warm a frozen connection when passion becomes cold.

Daisy's constant requests as things started to become heated caused my Daisy and I a little difficulty in bed. Her incessant requests resembled a thermostat with a 10 degree Celsius maximum setting. She insisted on certain things, so no matter how hard I tried to steam romanticism, it never got warm enough — most of the time, we ended up sleeping like rained-on logs.

You must continue practicing romance if you really want your soul mate to be committed to your union. Having a regular fitness routine is similar to practicing romance because without it, your muscles might tighten and your joints could become inflexible.

I spent a long time blaming Daisy for the decline of our relationship until my buddy dared to tell me that "it takes two to tango". This awakened me from my egoistic sleep and sent jittery goosebumps down my spine. Yes, I did give it some thought and painfully realized how much I, too, had contributed to the deteriorating friendship between Daisy and I. I came to see that Mom had a legitimate reason for bothering me at those busy times as it was the only time she could speak with me.

6. Continuing with that predictable trend

Nothing in a relationship, particularly when it comes to romantic inclinations, is more boring than an obviously predetermined pattern. A surprise for your soul partner would be wonderful.

One of the life lessons I picked up early on was seeing how my father used to surprise not just my mother but also my siblings and myself. He was one of those individuals who fully appreciated the power of mystery. He could abruptly end a party; drive us around only to realize that we are in a park; prepare a nice family dinner only to surprise us with holiday trip tickets requiring us to board a flight in the next two hours; set up nice drinks only to pour bitter aloe Vera juice extracts into our glasses; make us anticipate a wonderful Christmas day only to bring the bitter lemon juice and declare it a day of fasting, among many other things. Yes, he was full of surprises; you never knew what to anticipate.

My father taught me this lesson, which I put into practice quite well. Yes, the mystery attracted my beauty queens to me since they thought I was absolutely extraordinary, but the difference was created by little, every day surprises.

7. allowing actual volcanic explosions to occur in your mental flaws

The environment in which we live, as well as our upbringing, culture, and experiences, all influence our opinions. We all experience these factors to differing degrees, therefore it is inevitable that our perspectives on love, finding our soul mate, the future, and other issues will differ.

As a result, your soul partner and you will unavoidably have different perspectives on each interaction you have. The gender gap could potentially make this disparity in attitudes more pronounced. It seems sense that women would view partnerships somewhat differently than males.

To connect our attitudes with the highest expectations for our relationship, we must learn to mold them.

8. A wild seed is a "lazing" around thinking connection.

Only shrubs have wild seeds, which may at best be advantageous to primates. However, nothing comes to us as humans on a silver platter. It requires effort on your part. Relationships are not "lazy" affairs. It's a situation that requires ongoing attention. Relationships are not like a wild seed that is allowed to fend for itself in its own game of survival when it falls to the ground.

I told you how every time I played, I lost. Yes, I used to put a lot of effort into sowing untamed seeds in the name of beauty queens and would hope our relationship would flourish despite the fact that I never cared to water it. Later on, all of them faded, and I was unable to gather any ripe fruit—a soul mate.

You must continue to look after your connection. The weeds of difficulties are always vying for our nutrients of carelessness as we continue to develop. We must take care of the garden of our love lest what is left be eaten by weeds. In essence, starving your soul mate through neglecting your connection. The joys, passion, and love eventually fade as a result of being outweighed by difficulties that bloom when you forget to take care of your one valuable commodity in life—the garden of love.

9. reneging on your commitment to your true partner

Your soul mate's assurance of a brighter future together can only come through fidelity guarantee. If you betray it, your soul mate is lost. You could still be physically or emotionally connected, but it doesn't always indicate a soul connection still exists.

Lack of faithfulness on my side was one of my biggest failings that caused me to keep on losing my beauty queens. Lack of loyalty was more a product of my own insecurity, which led me to feel that I needed to diversify my risks by having many beauty queens. I would always think to myself, "Yes, I knew this was coming," as soon as one left the stable."And the more I continued to bolster my insecurities with more lady pals, the more I continued to lose. For me, it was such a challenging game.

Your soul mate connection should be founded on the highest level of good faith. You should have trust in your soul mate just as much as they do in you. Your own faithfulness, not that of your soul mate, serves as the guarantee blanket for your union.

10. Always having "big eyes"—the heightened jealousy

One of the primary illnesses that destroys many relationships is jealousy. Extreme jealousy is a symptom of the mental condition known as inferiority complex. The likelihood of your relationship progressing smoothly when your possible soul mate learns that you have this sickness is nearly nonexistent.

In terms of my interactions with my girlfriends, I was a really envious person. I've always worried that someone is attempting to usurp my position as beauty queen. Even though I pretended to give them permission to hang out with my guys, I couldn't help but feel uneasy. I consistently lost the majority of my beauty queens because of my envy. I would think about ditching someone if I saw them hanging out a lot with one of my buddies.

In relationships, jealousy is often a result of both insecurity and suspicion. Yes, I had suspicions that my beauty queens may be engaging in adultery in a similar manner to how I was. Had my beauty queens been protected from the same, my enmity may have been put to rest. However, they shared my concerns and were envious of my friendships with other women. The way Agnes handled herself in our relationship helped me get over my jealously. She never questioned me or worried about who I was dating. I also learned from this to stop worrying about who she was hanging out with. My fears eventually died a natural death due to our shared understanding.

11. retaining ungraciousness

We grow and feed the sickness of ingratitude every single day in our own unappreciative behaviors. The key to happiness is learning to appreciate the things in life; without it, pleasure will elude you and happiness will become a far-off illusion.

I had a terrible attitude with my girlfriends. I interpreted it as though they were fatefully my and hence entitled to be mine. I did not consider them a gift that came my way. Because of the loneliness I experienced every time I lost someone, I was constantly reminded that their presence in my life and the moments they spent with me were blessings rather than rights that I could exercise as I pleased.

Most of the time, ungratefulness is brought on by an attitude of entitlement. Whatever happens to you—for better or worse—is an opportunity that presents you with fresh options. The most moral thing to do is to learn to be thankful for everything that occurs. But if you can't see the positive in everything that occurs, you'll never develop this mentality.

12. always working like a goat

It is well known that goats are such creatures with practically the exact opposite traits as sheep. Goats usually want to do things alone unless it is unavoidable, but sheep always try to do things together.

I was such a he-goat, expecting my partner to always do what I said. I always wanted them to follow my orders, but I wasn't ready to do so since

I thought it would be too low. My ego was so nasty and deep.

You must act like sheep in a partnership by consulting and resolving to go together rather than simply going your own way since there is a method so that you may bravely face whatever is ahead.

PLAYER TENDENCIES

What to look out for: His present behavior will reveal his ambitions for the future. It will take some time to watch and observe his behaviors to make sure he is really genuine. Everyone of a sort conceals their identities, but when will the seams start to show?

Some males have an innate desire to flirt. They are who they are, after all. There's nothing wrong with it. However, when he goes out with the guys, he finds that they are either single or simply regular dudes in relationships. He feels the need to go out with them often and justifies it by stating that he is seeing his pals. He'll inevitably lie and cheat! When you and him are arguing, he will remark that he has to go outside and clear his thoughts. Because of this, he is already comfortable in the setting of appealing women. Regardless of what anybody claims, 90% of individuals who are in a crowd, particularly at a bar, are there to attract persons of the opposite sex.

if he permits you to daydream. He shows interest in you for a moment before vanishing. as soon as you hear from him. He gives off the vibe of being a tormented soul. He may say something like this. I haven't been in contact since I've been thinking a lot recently. He can add, "I've been putting a lot of effort into our future." He can claim that after our last date, he assumed you would need some distance and that you weren't interested in him. He can claim that since I've been betrayed previously and find it difficult to trust, I'm extremely cautious about letting people into my life. He could admit that he is falling for you and is unsure of how to handle the situation.

Players who cheat are adept at identifying the problem, so they will only tell you what you want to hear.

depending on the kind of person you are. He could have traits similar to yours. Many women are fervently seeking romantic relationships. Men are content to be alone if they can find sex elsewhere and don't need to be in a relationship. If he moves so quickly when you first start dating him and he is already making plans for your future. Everything you want to hear from him is being spoken. He's either in need or merely wants to have a bed with you. Without getting to know you first, how can you hope to develop anything? You need strong foundations if you want to develop anything. Or, on the other side, he will help someone else if he is prepared to leap over huddles for you. Thus, you are not unique! as he'll put it!

If he just concluded a protracted connection with his ex and has now discovered you. You develop a stronger emotional bond with someone the longer you are together. It just doesn't go that quickly. With pets, people develop attachments. We are referring to humans! We're talking about old habits being broken and odd, humorous gestures. Don't spend your time since it's likely that you're the rebound. Depending on how long he was involved in the prior relationship, it can take more than two weeks—possibly even two years. He needs some time to collect his thoughts and rediscover his identity. If he broke up with his ex after having an affair with you. Your relationship is doomed from the start since neither of you has any values.

It makes no difference how long you've known him. if he doesn't offer you his undivided attention, particularly at first in the relationship. For instance, when you are out with him and he keeps looking at his phone or staring at other ladies. He's going to defraud. You're just there to serve his wants while he searches for a new victim. Your time is not valuable to him, and he has no interest in collaborating with you.

He may forget his wallet while you're out on a date. Before leaving the house, every man makes sure their wallet is still in their possession. All males! Or perhaps he does carry his wallet and is just being stingy. This is a clear sign of what will happen next. Who are YOU, when he won't spend money on himself?

He is engaged to poverty and only he can divorce poverty before he can engage with you. His priorities are all wrong he should be looking to better his circumstances and yours.

Someone people are to open and honest from the beginning of the relationship. It takes time to gauge who the other person is. It is good to be honest and open, but he could you this to manipulate you as he already knows your weaknesses. Players always listen to everything so they can play to their advantages. Be careful all your doing is giving a template for him to follow to get what he wants from you. History can easily repeat itself unless you learn from it. Some women keep going on and on about being single. This is massive sign you don't want to be alone. You are not here to give your self-way. You're here to find the right companion. He will call you every day to make you laugh making you believe there is something special between you. He already knows you want somebody.

www.ingramcontent.com/pod-product-compliance
Lightning Source LLC
Chambersburg PA
CBHW050232120526
44590CB00016B/2056